Our Solar System

THE OUTER PLANETS

Mary-Jane Wilkins
Consultant: Giles Sparrow, FRAS

9 11 2 0 0 0 0 3 6 2 3 7 0

Published in paperback in 2017 by Wayland

© 2017 Brown Bear Books Ltd

Wayland
An imprint of Hachette Children's Group
Part of Hodder & Stoughton
Carmelite House
50 Victoria Embankment
London EC4Y 0DZ
An Hachette UK Company
www.hachette.co.uk
www.hachettechildrens.co.uk

ISBN 978 1 5263 0290 8

Brown Bear Books Ltd
First Floor, 9–17 St. Albans Place
London N1 0NX

Author: Mary-Jane Wilkins
Consultant: Giles Sparrow, Fellow of the Royal
Astronomical Society
Picture Researcher: Clare Newman
Illustrations: Supriya Sahai
Designer: Melissa Roskell
Design Manager: Keith Davis
Editorial Director: Lindsey Lowe
Children's Publisher: Anne O'Daly

Picture Credits
Front Cover: ©Shutterstock/Tristan 3D/Marcel
Clemens
Inside: 1, ©Shutterstock/Vadim Sadocski;
4, ©Shutterstock/Marcel Clemens; 4-5,
©Shutterstock/Mopic; 6, ©Shutterstock/
Jaroslava V; 6-7, ©Shutterstock/Maceij Sojka;
8, ©Shutterstock/Mr Timmi ; 8-9, ©NASA/JPL; 10,
©Shutterstock/Mode List; 10-11, ©NASA/Stephen
Groment; 12, ©NASA/JPL; 12-13, ©Shutterstock/
Jaan-Martin Kuusmann; 14, ©NASA/JPL/STScI;
14-15, ©Shutterstock/Mr Timmi ; 16, ©NASA/
JPL-USGA; 16-17, ©NASA/JPL; 18bl, ©NASA/JPL-
Caltech; 18br, ©EPA/I/Calcada & Nick Risinger
(skysurvey.org); 18-19, ©NASA/JHUAPL/SWRI;
20, ©NASA/JHUAPL/SWRI; 20-21, ©NASA/JPL; 23,
©NASA/JPL/DLR.
T=Top, C=Centre, B=Bottom, L=Left, R=Right

Brown Bear Books has made every attempt
to contact the copyright holder. If you have
any information please contact:
licensing@brownbearbooks.co.uk

Websites
The website addresses (URLs) included in this
book were valid at the time of going to press.
However, it is possible that contents or addresses
may change following the publication of this
book. No responsibility for any such changes
can be accepted by either the author or the
Publisher.

Contents

Where are the outer planets?

The outer planets are the four planets furthest away from the Sun. They are Jupiter, Saturn, Uranus and Neptune. They are all very cold places.

Outer planets

WOW!

Neptune is the planet furthest from the Sun. It is about 4.5 billion km away.

These planets are also called the gas giants. They are mainly liquid and gas, and they have no land.

The outer planets are beyond the asteroid belt. This is where most of the space rocks called asteroids come from.

Asteroid belt

Inner planets

Sun

5

The solar system

In the centre of our solar system is the Sun. The Sun is a star. It sends out the heat and light we call sunshine.

Mars

Jupiter

Rocky asteroids fly around the Sun, too.

Mercury

Venus

Earth

Earth's Moon

Eight planets circle (or orbit) the Sun. Mercury, Venus, Earth and Mars are closest to the Sun. Jupiter, Saturn, Uranus and Neptune are further away. Dwarf planets also orbit the Sun. Pluto is a dwarf planet. The Sun, planets and other space objects make up the solar system.

Uranus

Neptune

Pluto (dwarf planet)

Saturn

Moons and rings

The outer planets have lots of moons. Jupiter has the most. It has 67 moons! Saturn has 62 moons. Uranus has 27, and Neptune has 14. Scientists are finding new moons all the time.

WOW!

Ganymede is the biggest moon in the solar system. It is one of Jupiter's moons. The moon is bigger than the planet Mercury!

All the outer planets have rings around them, too. Saturn has the biggest, brightest rings. The rings around Jupiter, Uranus and Neptune are harder to see.

Jupiter

Jupiter is the biggest planet in the whole solar system. It has a layer of gases around it called an atmosphere. The gases form thick red, brown and yellow clouds.

Galileo

This is the Great Red Spot. It is a giant storm on Jupiter that is three times bigger than Earth!

Jupiter is very cold, windy and stormy. In 1995 a spacecraft called *Galileo* reached the planet. It spent eight years looking at Jupiter and its moons. Then it ran out of fuel and crashed.

WOW!

Jupiter is so big you could fit more than 1,300 Earths inside it.

Saturn

Saturn is the second biggest planet in the solar system. Like the other three gas giants, it is a very cold place.

A spacecraft called *Cassini* is studying Saturn's rings and moons.

Saturn has seven big rings around it.
Each is made from thousands of smaller rings.
These are made of pieces of ice and rock.
Some pieces are tiny and some are as big
as a house. They shine because sunlight
reflects off them like millions of mirrors.

Uranus

This planet looks different from the other seven planets. It seems to be tipped on its side. This means Uranus has very long days and nights. In some places they both last for 42 years!

Uranus looks different because it spins on its side.

The gases around Uranus make it look blue. It is the coldest planet in the solar system. It has 13 rings, but they are hard to see.

Like all planets, Uranus spins. Because it is tipped over, it spins in the opposite direction to Earth and most other planets.

Neptune

Neptune is further away from the Sun than any other planet in the solar system. It is dark, cold and very windy. The wind can blow at 1,000 kph!

Neptune

This photo was taken by a space probe called *Voyager 2*. It shows Neptune seen from its biggest moon, Triton.

The gases around Neptune make it look blue, like Uranus. There are six rings around it, but they are hard to see.

Triton

Voyager 2

Triton is one of the coldest places in the solar system. The temperature there is −240˚C.

Dwarf planets

Neptune is the furthest planet from the Sun.
But there are icy dwarf planets even further
from the Sun. A planet has its own orbit.
A dwarf planet shares its orbit with other
objects. These might be comets or asteroids.

WOW!

A spacecraft
called *Dawn* is
taking photos
of a dwarf planet
called Ceres.

Pluto

Scientists once thought Pluto was a planet. In 2006, they decided that it is a dwarf planet.

Eris

Scientists have found four other dwarf planets. Eris is a dwarf planet far beyond Pluto. It was discovered in 2005.

Exploring the outer planets

The outer planets are a long way from Earth. It takes years to reach them. Scientists sent two space probes to explore them in 1977. The probes were *Voyager 1* and *Voyager 2*.

In 2006, scientists launched a probe called *New Horizons*. It flew by Pluto in 2015 and sent back the first photos of Pluto to Earth.

The probes flew past all four outer planets. Then they flew on into space. In 2013 *Voyager 1* flew out of the solar system. The two probes will go on working until 2025.

Voyager 1

Make a Jupiter collage

What you need

Picture of Jupiter
Paper plate
Pencil

Red, cream and white
  dried beans
Glue
Sheet of black cardboard

What to do

1. Look at the picture of Jupiter. Draw lines on the plate to show where the different colours go. Leave a space for the Great Red Spot.

2. Sort the beans into different colours.

3. Glue the beans to the plate.

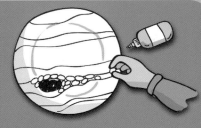

4. When you have filled the plate, leave it to dry.

5. Stick your collage onto black cardboard and hang it up!

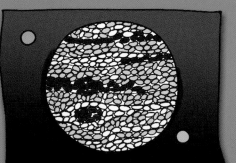

Useful words

asteroid
A big rock that orbits the Sun. An asteroid can be just a few metres across, or hundreds of kilometres wide.

atmosphere
The layer of gases around a planet, moon or star.

comet
A ball of rock, dust and ice that orbits the Sun.

dwarf planet
A small planet that does not have its own orbit.

moon
An object in space that orbits a planet. Not all planets have moons. Earth has one big moon. Other planets have lots of moons.

orbit
To move around another object.

planet
A large object in space that orbits the Sun or another star.

Sun
The star at the centre of the solar system.

Find out more

Websites

www.esa.int/esaKIDSen/
Planetsandmoons.html

www.kidscosmos.org/space_
center.php

www.planetsforkids.org/index.html

Books

First Fabulous Facts Space,
Anita Ganeri (Ladybird, 2014)

Little Kids First Big Book of Space,
Catherine D. Hughes (National
Geographic, 2012)

Index